The Girl Who Said She Could

Chantal Triay

The Girl Who Said She Could
Copyright © 2020 by Chantal Triay
All Rights Reserved.

Illustrations by Anne Potter
Book Design by Clarity Designworks

www.TheGirlWhoSaidSheCould.com

There once was a young girl with big dreams.

She dreamt of many, many things…

Things she thought could only happen in dreams.

**Sometimes,
she dreamt she had wings.**

Sometimes, she dreamt she was fearless.

"I can win this race."

**Sometimes,
she dreamt she was courageous.**

**Sometimes,
she dreamt she was innovative.**

Sometimes,
she dreamt she could buy
anything she wanted.

Sometimes,
she dreamt she was a hero.

Sometimes,
she dreamt she was creative.

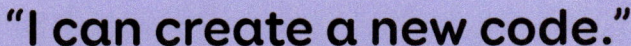

"I can create a new code."

Sometimes,
she dreamt she was brave.

Sometimes, she dreamt she could solve problems.

Sometimes,
she dreamt she could build great things.

"I can build that building."

Sometimes,
she dreamt she was tough.

**Sometimes,
she dreamt she was powerful.**

**Sometimes,
she dreamt she was convincing.**

Sometimes,
she dreamt she could
go above and beyond.

But when the sun came up and she opened her eyes, she realized those were not just dreams...

All of the things she dreamed of being were within her all along.

She knew she could become anything she wanted by believing in herself.

So, with one foot in front of the other, she began her journey and said, "I am ready to live my dreams."

What amazing things will you do?
Draw below

Activities
Can you do it? Let's see!

CHEMISTRY
What do you get when you mix sodium (Na+) and chloride (Cl-)?

a. Salt
b. Vinegar
c. Pepper
d. Ketchup

MATHEMATICS
16 + 13 = _____
27 - 18 = _____
15/3 = _____
22 x 4 = _____

PHYSICS
What kind of eclipse do we have when the moon is between the sun and the earth?

a. A Nuclear Eclipse
b. A Halloween Eclipse
c. A Solar Eclipse
d. A Space Eclipse

FUN FACTS: DID YOU KNOW?

There are about 1,000,000,000,000,000,000,000 (1 billion trillion) stars in the observable universe.

The Anglo-Zanzibar War of 1896 is the shortest war in history; it lasted only 38 minutes.

Some tornadoes can have wind speeds over 300 miles per hour, which is faster than the fastest race car!

You can survive for 3 MINUTES without oxygen or in icy water.

You can survive for 3 HOURS without shelter in a cold or hot environment.

You can survive for 3 DAYS without water.

You can survive for 3 WEEKS without food if you have water and shelter.

Answers: CHEMISTRY: a. Salt • MATHEMATICS: a. 29, b. 9, c. 5, d. 88 • PHYSICS: c. A Solar Eclipse

About the Author

Chantal Triay is a French-Mexican American who lives in Southern California and works as a Construction Engineer. She is an international guest speaker and published author, focusing on empowering girls and women around the world. Chantal is an avid community leader and has gained worldwide recognition for her inspirational influence.

This book is dedicated to those who dream, then dare to pursue those dreams.